# The Beginner's Bible
# Amazing Miracles of the Bible

## Sticker & Activity Book

**ZONDERkidz**

Copyright © 2022 by Zonderkidz

Requests for information should be addressed to:
Zonderkidz, 3900 Sparks Drive SE, Grand Rapids, Michigan 49546

ISBN 978-0-310-14158-7

Design: Diane Mielke

Printed in the United States

22 23 24 25 26 /CWM/ 6 5 4 3 2 1

# The World Is a Miracle

God made everything. It was all good. Use stickers to
finish this picture showing God's world.

# God Made Animals

God created the world and everything in it. He made animals!
Use stickers to finish this picture of God's amazing animals.

# Out of Egypt

Moses was helping God. He was leading the Israelites out of Egypt. The Red Sea was blocking their way. What an amazing miracle—the Red Sea parted! There was a dry path for the Israelites to escape.

Go through the maze to help Moses and the Israelites leave Egypt.

# What's the Difference?

God's people were in the desert. They were looking for the Promised Land.
They were so hungry. God sent food from the sky called manna.

Look at the pictures. Find 7 differences. Circle them.

# Jericho's Walls Fall

Joshua needed a miracle. He needed God's help to take Jericho. God made sure Joshua and his army would win. The army marched. They blew horns. The walls came tumbling down! God's miracle helped the army win!

Use stickers to finish the picture.

SUN

TALL

WALL

## Listen to God

Joshua and his army had to listen. God told them what to do. The WALL would FALL.

Read the words. Circle what rhymes with ALL.

Put stickers by the words that rhyme with ALL.

BALL

PAUL

TOOL

# God Provides

Elijah asked a woman for some bread and water. She said, "I have only enough for me and my son." Elijah said, "God will provide." Her oil and flour never ran out!

Complete the patterns below using three stickers in each row.

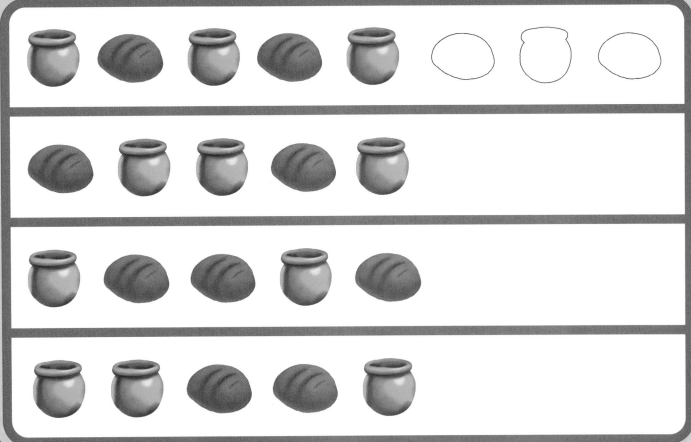

# The Fiery Furnace

The king said, "When you hear music, bow to me!" Three special men said, "No! We bow to God." The king threw them in a fiery furnace. Would they burn up? No, God saved them! He sent an angel to help them.

Finish the crossword puzzle.

Use the words below.

**King**

**Angel**

**Hot**

**Three**

## ACROSS

**2.** Who said to throw the men into the fiery furnace?

**3.** How many men were thrown into the furnace?

## DOWN

**1.** Who was in the furnace with the men?

**4.** The king said, "Make the furnace extra _____."

Now finish this picture with stickers. How many people did the king see in the fiery furnace?

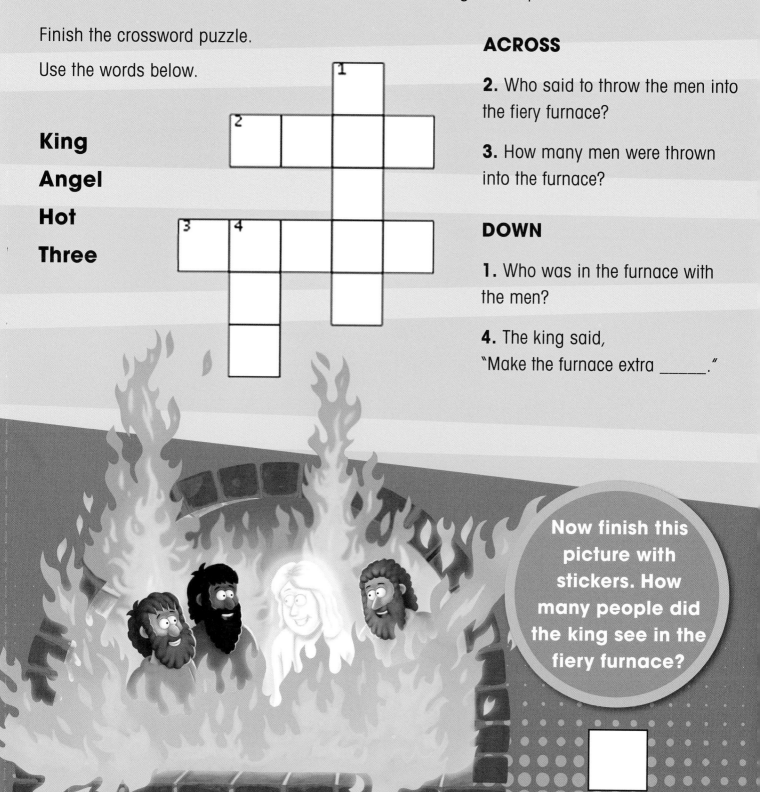

# Daniel and the Lions

The king said, "All people must pray to me!"
Daniel loved God. He prayed only to God.
The king put Daniel in the lions' cave. God
saved Daniel.

**Follow the outline and connect the dots. Color to finish the picture.**

# Jesus's First Miracle

Jesus performed his first miracle at a wedding. His mother saw the people were out of wine. She told Jesus to help. He listened to his mother. He turned jars of water into wine for the party.

Find 10 words in the puzzle.
Use the word bank to help.

**JESUS**

**MARY**

**MIRACLE**

**DISCIPLES**

**WEDDING**

**WATER**

**WINE**

**GOD**

**LOVE**

**CANA**

| X | M | A | R | Y | B | V | W | W | C |
|---|---|---|---|---|---|---|---|---|---|
| G | E | E | J | M | D | Q | I | E | A |
| O | G | K | T | P | I | C | N | D | N |
| D | H | J | G | B | S | M | E | D | A |
| W | A | T | E | R | C | I | A | I | A |
| N | R | A | J | V | I | R | I | N | N |
| Q | Y | Q | B | L | P | A | R | G | J |
| J | E | S | U | S | L | C | U | G | V |
| B | N | Z | H | E | E | L | O | V | E |
| S | Q | W | C | N | S | E | A | B | K |

# Loaves and Fishes

Many people were listening to Jesus teach. They all were hungry. A boy shared 5 loaves of bread and 2 small fish. Jesus blessed the food. It was enough to feed everyone and have some left! It was a miracle!

**Find the differences between the two pictures. Circle 6 things that are different.**

# Jesus Walks on Water

There was a big storm. Jesus's friends were scared.
Jesus walked out on the water so he could help them.
Look at the picture. Complete 1–5 below.

1. Add a lightning sticker in the sky.   2. Add two fish stickers to the water.

3. Put a red heart sticker on Jesus.   4. Circle the men who are scared of the storm.

5. Add a sticker of Peter, who is smiling at Jesus.

13

# Jesus Heals the Lepers

There were 10 lepers who asked Jesus to help them. They had a skin disease and it hurt. Jesus healed them all! Only one went back to say, "Thank you, Jesus!"

How many of the men did Jesus love? Put a heart sticker above the heads of the men Jesus loved.

# Lazarus Is Alive!

Jesus's friend Lazarus died. Jesus was sad. He prayed to God.
Lazarus was raised from the dead. It was a miracle!

Which path takes Jesus to his friend Lazarus? Trace the path with a crayon or marker.

# He Is Risen

Jesus rose from the dead on Easter morning! It was a miracle!
He visited his friends to tell them,
"I love you."
Find 8 words in the puzzle.
Use the word bank to help.

**JESUS**

**ALIVE**

**LOVE**

**ANGEL**

**TOMB**

**PEACE**

**EASTER**

**RISEN**

```
D J B P A L I V E L
T Z U Q O R I S E N
O J M T P E V O L X
M S K E A S T E R X
B X Q O W U Q D S L
L L A N G S M D I C
Z F A N G E L A S D
A S S O R J E Q W X
O D K A W A T G P F
N Q K G Q E C A E P
```